Becoming Wholehearted, A Journey into Authenticity

Darrell Cocup

Becoming Wholehearted, A Journey into Authenticity.

© Copyright 2025 Darrell Cocup

All rights reserved. No part of this publication may be reproduced, stored in a retrieval system, or transmitted in any form by any means – for example electronic, photocopy, recording – without the prior permission of the author.

For all further details contact darrell@wonderfullyfree.org

Cover design and typesetting by Laura Naioko

This book is dedicated to our lifesaving friends, you know who you are! Gracias!

Thanks

A huge 'Thank you' to all those on our wonderful Sozo team who took the trouble and care to read through my manuscript and make comments, suggestions and corrections, you're all very special! Thanks too to Chris Wright for correcting grammar and typos and to Margaret, Susan and Paul for their invaluable editorial comments!

"Oh, the depth of Satan! He wants to put men off with mere head knowledge of Christ and salvation, and have them rest there and go no further."
Isaac Ambrose, The Christian Warrior, 1662.

The Heart: The core of our being that reflects the absolute essence of who we truly are. It is the seat of our emotions and feelings, serving as the bridge to our authentic emotional connection with ourselves. To be truly connected, we must allow ourselves to fully feel and authentically express our emotions, embracing the heart's wisdom as a guide to self-awareness, wholeness and authenticity.

Foreword

The most important journey for every one of us is to have a WHOLE HEART. In leading us on a journey of authenticity, with ourselves, God, and others, Darrell is giving us tools to achieve that goal.

Simple phrases that include reference to our hearts often carry an assumption that we all have a similar understanding. This book helps to move us closer to an understanding that is both applicable and achievable.

Darrell gives a great resource to get started on a journey of inner healing, or a great follow up tool, to reinforce the breakthroughs we receive in the 'counsellors chair' I commend it to you.

As I write these few sentences I am also conscious of the man behind the words which I am endorsing. He is himself sincere, and integrous. His ability to be vulnerable and authentic, hungry for more of God, and more insight into himself and a genuine love of people, desiring others to get their breakthrough, qualifies him to write to the rest of us, encouraging our journey of authenticity, hunger for God, self-acceptance and love.

May you be blessed as you read and act upon the advice, and may others around you enjoy your whole heart.

Paul Manwaring
Fathering People and Organisations
Bethel author
paulmanwaring.com

Contents

Preface	10
Day One : Anyone Who Had a Heart …and not taking it for granted	13
Day Two: Emotions and Feelings…and getting to understanding them	17
Day Three: Heartbreak…and what that can mean	21
Day Four: Surprise…head and heart and the difference	25
Day Five: Our Hearts Tell Our Stories…feelings and the truth	29
Day Six: And So…the other side of the story	33
Day Seven: When One Thing Leads to Another…responding to life's circumstances	37
Day Eight: Trauma…how things in the past can affect us	41
Day Nine: So What?…what have we learned, where is this going?	45
Day Ten: Cause and Effect…our life's bigger picture	49
Day Eleven: Going Deeper…how what you think affects the rest of you	53
Day Twelve: At Last!: Exploring the healing in forgiveness	57
Day Thirteen: Emotional Baggage…unpacking the pain of the past	61
Day Fourteen: …and how to deal with it	65
Day Fifteen: Going Through Forgiveness…learning to hear from your heart	69
Day Sixteen: I Choose to Forgive…how to forgive and really mean it	73

Day Seventeen: Finding Your Higher Power…who really answers those deep questions? ……… 77

Day Eighteen: Why Would He Bother? …a challenge for the truth ……… 81

Day Nineteen: A relationship of Love…discovering God's love for you ……… 85

Day Twenty: Why Choose God?...can God really be trusted? ……… 89

Day Twenty-One: What's the Point?...Where's this all taking me? ……… 93

Day Twenty-Two: Simply You: Finding who we're meant to be ……… 97

Day Twenty-Three: 'Positives' and 'Negatives'…learning to be true to yourself ……… 101

Day Twenty-Four: The Benefit of Happiness…where do you sit on the 'happy scale'? ……… 105

Day Twenty-Five: Going Back to Roots…the behaviours we've carried from childhood ……… 109

Day Twenty-Six: Just a Few More…the problem with guilt or shame ……… 113

Day Twenty-Seven: Bringing it All Back Home (Part One)…understanding the impact of family ……… 117

Day Twenty-Eight: Bringing it All Back Home (Part Two)…understanding the impact of environment ……… 121

Day Twenty-Nine: It's All About Balance: how to be at peace with yourself ……… 125

Day Thirty: Living the Destination: learning to be authentic ……… 129

Day Thirty-One: Finale: 'knowing yourself is true wisdom' ……… 133

Preface

There's a school of thought that would tell us that it's a good thing to let our heads (rationality) rule our hearts (our emotions), because that's the sensible, right and proper way for life to be run. Then there are those, possibly more romantic amongst us, who tell us to let our hearts rule our heads, the idea being that life will be more spontaneous and exciting, risky almost, if we do this. Again, there's been much written about the 18" journey that lies between our head and our heart, making one the destination of the other. The Sioux believed this to be the longest journey we can make in life. Michael Formica, writing in Psychology Today, tells us that taking something we know in our heads and turning it into action, something that will elicit change in our hearts and therefore in our lives and the lives of those around us, is true wisdom, giving the journey more of a point and a reason. And so it goes on, with lots of different views and wisdom circling this most complex of subjects, the relationship between our head and our heart.

Our view, and the one explained and unpacked in the 31 daily thoughts that follow, is that there is indeed a journey, but one that takes place within our hearts. It's a journey of 'getting-to-know', of developing relationship and of trusting our heart so that we become able to live our lives from the richness of our true feelings and emotions rather than from the cold head knowledge and self-beliefs instilled by our pasts. Our hearts are then a safe informant for our heads to listen and respond to.

There's a caveat, though, which is that one's heart needs to be healed, or, in other parlance, 'made whole' before one's head can benefit from what it carries. And, just to complicate things, one's head can carry ideas that one's heart feels differently about, and so, on this journey, there has to be some to-ing and fro-ing between the two. One thing is unarguable, that to be emotionally connected to ourselves we have to be able to authentically feel and express our emotions. Doing so allows others to see, know and support us as we need them to.

And then there's the question of what success in this journey looks like. We'd say that success is being whole-hearted, and that being wholehearted means living a truly authentic life…a life knowing and living confidently out of one's true and full identify. Are you ready for that? We hope so…

But Before you Start…

There's no rush! Although there are 31 'Days' in what follows, there's no need to hurry. It's important that you give yourself permission to miss days, and don't try and catch up in a rush if you do. You may decide to space this journey over a couple of months, or more or less. What matters is the change within.

Above all else, guard your heart, for everything you do flows from it.
Proverbs 4:23

DAY ONE   Date

Anyone Who Had a Heart… and not taking it for granted

Having a heart is a bit of an odd concept. We all have one. We depend on it, in fact, well, where would you be without yours? It's literally vital, yet we take it completely for granted, until, that is, it starts to play up. That's when we start to give it the attention it deserves. It's odd though, we only really feel it working when we put it under pressure, when we're labouring in some way. Just hold that thought, we'll be coming back to it.

What, though, of the heart of our emotions? There's a bit of mixed understanding here, after all, we talk about getting to the heart of a matter, and this suggests that we think of the heart of something as being the absolute kernel of it, the central point, that place where everything is concentrated. Which makes a 'heart' of any sort pretty important, at least it should, but then 'heart' in this usage is just acting as a reference point, it's not drawing us to think of why we use this word in this way…
…but perhaps it should, because all down through history, in every culture and language, the heart, our hearts, have been recognised as harbouring the absolute essence of who we are, our core, if you like. Now, you may have thought that it's our heads that do this, after all our heads hold what brains we have and it's our brains that do the thinking, but we believe that it's our hearts, somehow, that hold our emotions and feelings.

How does that work? Allow us to try and explain. When things happen to us in life, when an event takes place, good or bad, the memory of it remains in our brains, we can recall it, but somehow the emotions attached to that memory, how it made us feel, go straight to our hearts and stay there until we do something about them. Which, of course, we may not choose to do if the event was enjoyable and the memory a good one…but we might well want to do something about if the memory causes us pain or distress. And a final thought to tickle your grey cells on this first day. We'll be talking a lot about emotions and feelings, and it may sound like they're much the same thing. Think about it for a moment. Are the words interchangeable? If so, why have two words? We want to try and give some clarity as to what each of these are because you'll find it helpful for yourself to be aware of how you experience each of them.

Think of it like this. Right now, how are you feeling? You'll probably have to stop and think about it. Are you happy or sad or somewhere in between? Are you thirsty? Or bored? Or maybe all these at once? Whatever your feelings are, they are based on something much deeper, your emotions…

Thought Stop

Do you take your heart for granted? Have you ever been aware of it being capable of feelings, either emotional or physical, and, if so, how have you responded?

Activation

We've just asked you to think about how you're feeling right now. How's that going? Did you just read it and pass on? You'll have a choice in this book to either engage with the process or to read it as an outsider to critique. Obviously, it's up to you! You are, as they say, powerful and free to decide your approach, but we would love you to engage because we know that doing so will make a difference. How does that feel? What will be your approach?

The purposes of a person's heart are deep waters, but one who has insight draws them out.
Proverbs 20:5

DAY TWO

Emotions and Feeling…and getting to understand them

We don't want to get into semantics here, which it would be very easy to do. Google the two words 'emotions' and 'feelings' and many hours of reading later there's every chance you'll only be more confused. Here's what psychologist Ross Buck says. He distinguishes between three levels of emotional responses, handily called Emotion I, II and III, depending on the level we are conscious of them.

Emotion III is the level at which we have a conscious awareness of an emotional state. It's when we have a feeling, it could be anger, or joy or fear, but we're aware of it and we're aware of our body's response, which could be laughter, shivers or whatever.

Emotion II is made up of our emotional displays as seen by others, with or without our being aware of it. It's signalled through body language, in other words our mannerisms, tones of voice, gestures, facial expressions, brief touches, even the pauses in what we say. What's important here is that we are often oblivious to what we're communicating, and the people we're with often oblivious to the non-verbal messages they're picking up. Next time you're with someone, or in a group, try and distance yourself from the conversation and see what you're picking up about the person or people you're with purely through the way they are, not what's being said. You'll be amazed.

Emotion I is very subtle. Even as you're engaging with the people and situations around you, your body is responding physiologically to the emotional stimuli being in that situation is provoking in you. You don't know it's happening, but your nervous system is at work discharging chemicals; hormones are being produced and those immune system changes which activate our fight, flight, freeze or fawn mechanism, all are at work. It just happens automatically.

So, it's in the Emotion III state that we experience feelings, because feelings are the recognition of an emotional experience or a physical sensation, again, anger, joy or pain. Feelings are, by definition, a conscious experience.

Why is this important? What has this to do with our heart health? It's this: If our emotions are out of our control, if, for example, we have memories that cause us extreme pain or fear, then our bodies will constantly over-react. Our Emotion I chemicals will over-produce. We become sick because our bodies are out of what is called homeostasis, the balance of our internal, physical, and chemical conditions. It's literally vital for us to understand and be at peace with our emotions.

A large part of having that peace is achieving emotional competence, which really doesn't mean being like Mr Spock and remaining super cool at all times but does mean being able to feel our emotions and be aware of when they are causing us stress. There's another consideration: Are we responding to something purely in the present, or is something that is happening in the present triggering a reaction to something that happened in the past?

Lastly, having emotional competence also means being able to express our emotions effectively, able to assert our needs and keep emotional boundaries.

All to say that our heart health, our emotional peace, is central to our physical wellbeing.

Thought Stop

It's astonishing how unaware we are of so much of how we respond to life, good and bad. It's as if we're mostly on autopilot, only aware of what we're doing and what's going on around us at a superficial level. We can change this. The more aware we are of how we function at a subconscious level, the greater our levels of understanding and self-control will be. Perhaps just as importantly, the more we understand ourselves, the more we'll understand others.

Activation

Ask your heart a question and see what it says. Try something apparently simple, such as "Heart, how are you feeling?" and write down what you think it replies.

A happy heart makes the face cheerful, but heartache crushes the spirit.
Proverbs 15:13

DAY THREE

Date

Heartbreak...and what that can mean

We hope yesterday's explanation helped! It was a bit of a detour, but one we thought worth taking. On Day One we talked about how both our emotions and feelings are harboured in our hearts and on Day Two we challenged you to ask your heart a question and see what response you got. Did you try it? Were you surprised by the response you got? If you're of a slightly cynical nature you may think that any answer you got was just your mind playing tricks. If so, give it another go, no one is listening! It works, doesn't it, and the more often you talk to your heart the more two-way your 'conversation' will be, and the more in touch you will be with those emotions and feelings we keep going on about.

Be aware, though, that your heart may not be as ready to respond to you as you might think it should be. If your heart has had a hard time of it, if your feelings and emotions have been battered by life and misused, scared even, then it's not going to be ready to come out and 'act normal' in the way you might want, or even expect it to. We talk about heartbreak as being a response to disappointment in love, we go so far as to romanticise it, making heartbreak something wistful, a sort of necessary and inevitable by-product of a failed relationship. Sometimes we even make it no more than a period of sadness before the next love adventure, but a broken heart is so much more than this. Broken hearts, and a heart can be broken in more ways than just romantically, sometimes never recover; they can cause a person to hide from the world, unable to engage with it. Your heart not only holds your emotions and feelings, it has, in a way that we hope you'll get to understand, emotions and feelings of its own. Recognising this, and treating your heart as an entity in itself, will help you to get to know it, and ultimately yourself, more quickly and at a deeper level.

If it's any comfort, very few of us have got through life unscarred, without any heartache at all. Even if our parents have had the very best of intentions it would be very unusual if they managed to meet all our needs, and so we all carry elements of sadness or fear, in with, hopefully, experiences of joy and happiness. If your Dad was absent a lot of the time, for example, it may have been due to his working overseas, but the rejection we might have felt as a result will be very real to us, even if it's unfounded. And our heart will have suffered. There'll be more on this in Day Four.

Thought Stop

Hurt is very real. It can happen in a moment, and we can carry it for a lifetime. Sometimes we get so used to hurt that we allow it to become our justification and identity and, of course, the only person who's hurt by us carrying hurt…is us, and those around us we impact. Here's the good news, we can turn hurt into hope and carry that instead, but it takes us to understand the damage that hurt does to us to be able to reject it and turn to hope instead.

Activation

Without asking it, write down how you think your heart might be feeling, given what you know about your life. Is there hurt? What would it feel to live a life of hope?

_____

_____

_____

_____

_____

The best and most beautiful things in the world cannot be seen or even touched. They must be felt with the heart.
Helen Keller

DAY FOUR   Date

Surprise!...head and heart and the difference

How did you feel after reading yesterday's message? Did you perhaps feel a little 'spooked out' when you began to realise that there may be more going on in your heart than just pumping life through your veins? Did you begin to see there may be more to what happens in your heart than maybe you first thought?

We floated the idea yesterday that your heart not only holds your emotions and feelings but that it has emotions and feelings of its own. Perhaps a better way of putting this is to say that your heart holds its own reactions and responses to the emotions and feelings that whatever has happened in your life may have placed upon it. In that respect, and this may be hard to get your head around, it may know more about how the 'real' you is responding to life than the you that largely reacts to life out of our heads.

Really?
How can that be? Think of it like this: Your brain stores memories. If you Google 'where are memories held' you'll find that received wisdom tells us that the sort of long-term memories that we're talking about are initially kept in that part of your brain called the hippocampus and then, over time, become integrated into another part of your brain, the cerebral cortex, that bit responsible for the higher order functions that make us human. This process is referred to as cortical integration; it protects the information stored. So that's the flash-back picture memory type recall…but we tend to experience this a bit like play-back without sound. It's telling you what happened stripped of how it made you feel. The feelings and your emotional response to those feelings are stored in our hearts, so your head might tell you that when your primary school teacher told you that you were stupid and ridiculed you at the front of class it was just one of those things, it happened and you just lived with it and got over it, but ask your heart how it felt and the hurt and shame might well pour out. Your heart can tell a different truth to your head.

Here's the very important point. We respond to life out of our hearts. The hurt and shame felt as a result of that primary school teacher's actions will have caused us to believe things about ourselves, after all, if someone as important as a teacher tells us we're stupid then they must be right, mustn't they? And if I'm stupid then I should stay quiet, not have opinions, be un-worthy of love, and the list goes on. That front of class incident could influence, could totally change, the pattern of my life and, what's more, I could well live my life believing I'm stupid but not realising why it is I think this. And without it being even remotely true. So even if my head says that it's ridiculous to still feel stupid and to feel my opinions are worthless, I begin to realise that the real me is still living in reaction to (and with the consequences of) that school incident.
Now that's something to think about...

Thought Stop
The day-to-day life we live is the outcome of the culmination of all that's happened in it so far, good and bad. It's a bit like those 'join the dots' drawings children enjoy. Each memory that we retain is a dot and, joined together, they produce a picture of the influences on our life. It's more than just memories, though, it's impressions too. A childhood of poverty, of parental rows and/or of abuse or, on the other hand, of happy days and abundant love will also create the internal world we live from.

Activation
What's it like to hear that your heart might know more about the 'real' you than your head. How does it feel to read this? What emotions does it stir? Can you write them down?

_____

_____

_____

You can outdistance that which is running after you, but you cannot outdistance that which is running inside you.
African Proverb

DAY FIVE

Date

Our Hearts Tell Our Stories…feelings and the truth

If our hearts tell a different truth to our heads, then…what's the truth? Which is correct? The answer is probably…both, and at the same time, maybe neither. We're not trying to be clever here and certainly not controversial, because we're hoping you'll agree that absolute truth and our memories of what happened, (the truth to us), can differ. We remember things as we saw them at the time. Our memory may well tell us that Dad deserted us for long periods when we were very young, but the absolute truth may be that he was repeatedly ill, or working overseas, or in the Navy, in other words, that he didn't desert us, he just couldn't be there for us all the time. If we can accept that our memories represent our truth, i.e. our interpretation of the factual events that happened, then hopefully you can see how our hearts will hold the emotions and feeling that were created at the same time as the memory, and those emotions and feelings will reflect the truth of that memory as we understood it.
Let's take another look at Dad 'deserting' us. If the emotions and feelings our heart carries as a result of that memory are premised on his 'desertion' then, in our heart, we'll feel all the negative responses that come with being deserted, i.e. of being unwanted, abandoned, insufficient, in the way, and more. As a result, we may well carry emotions of rejection, of not being good enough, not being interesting, not worth investing in, and so it goes on. We'll judge ourselves too, allowing these things to become the truth of who we think we are. And if this sounds like a bit of a repeat of the primary school teacher from yesterday, it's just another example of how things can work out in our life.

Where is this taking us? Hopefully to the point of acceptance that, as today's heading tells us, our hearts tell our stories. They may not reflect or even be aware of the absolute truth of what has happened to us, but they can tell us of their own perception and understanding of what has happened, how it felt at the time, how it feels now, and the impact of it on our life in a way that our brains cannot.

What's important is that it's actually not so much what happens to us that matters but how that made us feel at the time - and the residual effect on our life.

Thought Stop

Hopefully, what the above is telling you is that very little in our life is written in stone and therefore can't be changed. We are a mishmash of memories, beliefs, judgements and responses and wisdom tells us that the more prepared we are to accept a change in perception and even direction, the more true to ourselves we will be.

Activation

What are the absolute certainties in your life? Those things you're sure of? How did your emotional reactions to events shape them, your beliefs and your behaviours?

> *The curious paradox is that when I accept myself just as I am, then I can change.*
> Carl Rogers

DAY SIX

And So...the other side of the story

Perhaps our closing comment yesterday was a little severe. Of course it matters what happens to us. If it didn't happen, we wouldn't have the attendant feelings and emotions. But whilst the memory is important (and can itself be deeply damaging, we'll look at that later), it's the feelings and emotions we want to work with. We've mentioned a couple of times how the responses stored in our hearts can affect us and how our perceptions of the truth of those responses can change the way we do life, and that's what we're considering today.

Let's go back to our primary school teacher and what we may have believed about ourselves as a result of him or her having ridiculed us at the front of class. Cause and effect being what it is, if we believe ourselves to be stupid, we're going to allow other people to treat us as being stupid. And each time someone treats us that way, as being stupid, it reinforces our own belief in our stupidity. But, whoa! let's look at this whole scenario. Let's go back to school and revisit that day at the front of class. Oh my goodness! Teacher's husband had left her the day before, or she had just found out she was being evicted, or her dog had died. She was having a bad day, she just took it out on you, not least because she felt you could take it. She didn't think you were stupid at all. By that afternoon she had forgotten all about it. Thirty years later, you haven't. And here's the saddest part of it. This area of your self-belief, a belief that has moulded your life all this time, is, in truth, based on a fundamental misconception and a lie. But here's the good news, it doesn't have to stay this way, lies can be revealed, exposed for what they are, and dealt with.

One other thing here. We are, all of us, emotionally complex beings. No one part of us works in isolation to the rest of us. The lie and wound about being stupid will inevitably have a knock-on effect in other areas of our life...and people will see that in us. If you have a broken leg, it's obvious. If you have a broken heart, a broken spirit, it's not. At least not so obvious, but people will still see it, even if not consciously. It will come out in your

Emotion II actions. Have you ever met someone and thought, "What a miserable person!" or worked with someone generally considered to be toxic? Those people are carrying wounds you can't see, but you can feel as you subconsciously recognise their Emotion II ways of expression. Some are a lot more obvious than others, but most of us carry them to some extent. Until, that is, we deal with them.

Thought Stop

Have you ever thought about what people see in you, the impression you make, the atmosphere you carry? You can't not carry an atmosphere, so what's yours? A good way to find out is to ask someone who cares for you. They may be a bit surprised by the question but if you explain to them what we covered on Day Two about emotions they'll soon get the picture. You may be surprised at what they tell you.

Activation

If you've acted on today's Thought Stop then your next step is to ask yourself what atmosphere you'd actually like to carry, presuming, that is, that it's a different one! You may have to make a few changes to the way you think and see yourself but it's completely possible. Make a note of the atmosphere you think you carry, how people perceive you, below, and then how you think the real you would be perceived and then see how you change to become more like the real you as you go through this book.

> *Give sorrow words; the grief that does not speak knits up the o'er wrought heart and bids it break.*
> Shakespeare, Macbeth.

DAY SEVEN

Date

When One Thing Leads to Another…responding to life's circumstances

We pick up where we left off, with the thought that an initial lie we believe about ourselves will have knock on effects. Let us for a moment assume that at some point today you'll be walking along, whistling a happy tune when suddenly you nearly knock someone over. "Bloody idiot, be more careful," they snarl at you before moving on. How do you respond?

It depends. If you're a confident person who believes in yourself and has a full measure of self-worth, you'll have apologised and then felt sorry for someone who gets so wound up about a simple mistake. On the other hand, if you already think you're an idiot you'll shrink inside as you receive yet another confirmation of the truth of it. If, on top of feeling an idiot, you're also fearful, you'll have either felt frozen to the spot, wanted to run away or to have chased the person and hit them, depending on how you respond to this threat that has provoked fear in you. The fear you feel will have a cause, a root. It may be as a result of that primary teacher again, or it may be the result of something quite different, or, and here's something to think about, it may be the outcome of something that happened after the primary school horror, something that would not have caused you any problems at all, had you not already had your life rocked by the problem of being told you're stupid.

There are two things we want to highlight here. One is the cumulative effect of wounds and lies, so that, in this case, being told you're stupid at the front of class and believing it has opened the door to other lies being readily accepted. On Day Three we mentioned that a belief that often goes hand in glove with the lie that we're stupid is that we're worthless. As a worthless person I hang back from involvement in things. As a worthless person my opinions don't matter, so I don't say much. Confrontation of any sort scares me. I'm a fearful person. Feeling stupid has had the effect of making me fearful. The initial lie has had several layers added to it, wreaking havoc in my life. So many of us have had our lives completely changed

in our impressionable childhood, either by one or a series of negative events that have left an indelible mark on who we believe we are, or simply by being brought up in a challenging and unsafe environment.
And the other…we'll get to cover tomorrow!

Thought Stop

Have you any fears? Do you know why you have them? Some people "are scared of their own shadows", why is that? And what if we have had no direct experience to cause us to be fearful, but we are. Fear, as with anger, anxiety and so many emotional responses can also be learned. If we had a fearful or angry parent displaying these behaviours as we grew up we can easily (and unintentionally) pick up these ways of doing life and make them our own.

Activation

Can you identify any fear-based behaviours in your own way of living life? Where did they come from? Are they yours, as a result of an experience, or did you learn them from a parent or other authority figure?

Trauma is not what happens to us, but what we hold inside in the absence of an empathetic witness.
Peter Levine

DAY EIGHT

Date

Trauma...how things in the past can affect us

Trauma isn't a word we've mentioned before. It carries with it overtones of extreme pain and suffering, even of the unspeakable, and yet trauma is what we've been speaking about every day so far. It's what this book you're reading is ultimately all about.

What would be your definition of the word 'trauma'? Here's what the UK mental health charity, Mind, says about it:
'Going through very stressful, frightening or distressing events is sometimes called trauma. When we talk about emotional or psychological trauma, we might mean:
- situations or events we find traumatic
- how we're affected by our experiences.

Traumatic events can happen at any age and can cause long-lasting harm. Everyone has a different reaction to trauma, so you might notice any effects quickly, or a long time afterwards.' Which just about covers it. But we're just going to add a further line of explanation, and it's this: a trauma is the origin of any retained negative memory that has caused us emotional wounding, either initially or long term. These can be an event but can also be the cumulative effect of living in an unsafe or unstable environment. Which makes sense when you think about it, because good memories don't wound us. If anything, they do quite the opposite, they encourage and give us self-strength. It's the negative memories that hurt.

How does knowing that we're talking about trauma help? Well, hopefully, it will act as an equaliser, and what we mean is that we'll realise and accept that one person's normal can be another person's major trauma. What has a deep and lasting effect on one person won't necessarily wound another. Another child may have taken teacher's behaviour at the front of class as being hardly worth a second thought. To our child it resulted in a life-to-date trauma, and a trauma is a trauma to the person carrying it, no matter how benign the origin may appear to anyone else.
Appreciating this and being open to understand another person's trauma

and how it has worked out in their lives is a considerable step towards understanding the trauma in our own. And let's be very clear about something here. There is absolutely no shame in carrying trauma, no matter how it was caused. There's no need to feel ashamed because something that means nothing to other people causes you to feel anxious or creates a need to escape. There is no shame in not having 'dealt with' a past trauma. Most of us don't even recognise either how a trauma experienced in our childhood has affected us, or, conversely, when our current behaviour is a direct result of that trauma. But you will if you keep reading!

Thought Stop

Many of us think that to experience a trauma a dramatic event must have occurred, but this isn't necessarily the case. Living in a traumatic atmosphere is in itself a trauma. Consult Dr Google for a definition and you'll find plenty. None appear to reflect something that's really important, which is the solitary nature of trauma. Trauma happens when there's no one to share the experience with, when the event feels uniquely one's own. Our nature is to compare our response with someone else's response to the same thing. If it's normal to them then our fear can subside to a level where the experience may well be appalling but not traumatic.

Activation

Reflect on what you've read over these last few days. Do you identify with any of it? How does doing so make you feel?

"For I know the plans I have for you," declares the LORD, *"plans to prosper you and not to harm you, plans to give you hope and a future.*
Jeramiah 29:11

DAY NINE

Date

So What?...what have we learned? Where is this going?

We're into our second week. Before going any further, let's recap.

We're suggesting:
• That our brains hold our memories, but that our hearts hold the emotions and feelings arising from those memories.
• That feelings are the expression of emotions.
• That we might ask the same question to our head, our brain and to our heart and get a different answer.
• That if we're not used to asking our hearts questions we may be out of touch with our feelings.
• That our feelings are a result of our perception of what happened in a memory.
• That our perception of the truth, what we believe, will dictate our reaction to that perception, and how we think and behave in life as a result.
• That negative memories have inevitably been traumatic in that the original event or life circumstances have wounded us.

What can we do about all of this?

Perhaps the first step is to accept that all of us carry trauma to some degree and that, as we concluded yesterday, the trauma we carry affects our everyday life in ways of which we may not be entirely, or indeed partially, aware. Of course, we may be fine with this and not want to be made aware of the degree to which our lives are compromised because of the effect of trauma. To many this is raking over burnt coals, it's bringing up a past that's, well, past; that horse has bolted, we feel, it's water under the bridge. Which sounds feasible, except it isn't true. It's never too late to deal with the past, and why would any of us want to hang on to those misconceptions and lies about ourselves a moment longer than we have to?

That question, why would any of us want to hang on to misconceptions and lies about ourselves was rhetorical, so forgive us for that. Our answer, and it's one you may not want to admit to, is, usually…fear. We hang on to those misconceptions and lies out of fear. It's almost invariably a fear of revisiting old hurts, of digging up memories that carry trauma from the past, trauma we think we've either dealt with or buried so deep that it can no longer hurt. I mean, why would anyone want to talk about / bring to the surface stuff that we've managed to bury deep all these years? And, perhaps on a deeper level, who will I be if I start to deal with everything I'm carrying?

And this isn't an unreasonable response, other than the fact that this 'stuff' has probably shaped you into being someone you were never meant to be. "I am what I am", some people say, "and there's no changing me." And that's another fear-based lie, because the truth is your life can be turned around completely, and without any need to be fearful…

Thought Stop

We always have a choice in life, we can continue to live it as we are, warts and all, or we can accept that there's a better version of us waiting to be discovered, nurtured and produced, not necessarily like a bunch of flowers being produced with a flourish from behind someone's back, but teased out gently as we recognise those things that we've just accepted as being 'us' that really aren't. Parting with the 'us' we know can be a challenge, after all, we've lived with 'us' for a long time, but if that 'us' is the product of past hurt and pain then surely it's better dealt with and left behind…and that's the choice.

Activation

What would you like your future to look like? Imagine yourself free of all life's troubles and stresses, how would that feel? What would you do?

Trauma is not just a mental experience, it can deeply affect our physical health, leaving lasting impacts on our bodies and overall well-being.
Dr Bessel van der Kolk

DAY TEN

Date

Cause and Effect...our life's bigger picture

Yes, it's true, you can confront your past, you can face it and deal with it and put it behind you and move on. It is possible to reset your life, to 'put your feet on higher ground' as Van Morrison puts it, and tomorrow we'll start to look at how...but for today...
...and without wanting to be like one of those interminable emails that try and sell you something without getting to the point of telling you what it is, allow us, just today, to paint for you a bigger picture of what trauma can do to us, other than mess with our identity and self-belief. It can also cause us significant, even fatal, health problems.

It is increasingly being recognised that our mental health and physical health cannot be treated separately as if there was no connection between the two. There's nothing new here, hundreds of years before Christ, the Greek philosopher, Socrates, noted a doctor's criticism of his fellow doctors, saying, "This is the reason why the cure of so many diseases is unknown...they are ignorant of the whole. For this is the great error of our day in the treatment of the human body, that physicians separate the mind from the body." So, there's nothing new in this idea of being holistic, but it's still a very little understood area of practice. Or maybe it's just a very unpractised area of practice!

This is perhaps not the time and place to start carping on about how modern medicine tends to treat the visible symptoms of illness and disease rather than being holistic and recognising that there's probably going to be a root to most sickness that needs to be addressed. And that we're all made up of three elements, body, mind and spirit. But!
How stressed do you feel? Honestly?

Thinking about getting to the root cause of sickness, would you agree that trauma almost inevitably causes stress? It does. And stress can cause havoc in our bodies, even, and maybe especially, the stress caused by childhood trauma that we hardly know we're carrying because it's so much a part of who we think we are, the us we've grown accustomed to being. Cancer, diabetes, arthritis, IBS, multiple sclerosis, immunological problems, the list of common diseases that are increasingly being recognised as having a root in suppressed or unrecognised stress originating in childhood is frightening. Not that it's our intention to frighten, what we want to do is emphasise that the first step to being free of the wounds of the past is to recognise where they came from and what they're doing in our life, and then to face them and, as we said on Day Five, deal with them!

Thought Stop

We talked the other day about our ability to make choices and when it comes to sickness, choices abound. There are those whose identity is built on their sickness, who, without saying a word, are crying out, "I'm a victim, look at me", but these are the exception in that most of us would prefer to be sickness free. The choice is how we handle this and, actually, it's sometimes less of a choice than we may think because, in essence, we're programmed by our past experiences to think and act as we do. It will be down to whether you're a 'glass half full' or 'glass half empty' sort of person and we'll either treat our sickness as something we can beat and get over or as something catastrophic and insurmountable. The good news is that this takes us back to choice. Whatever our natural default thinking may be about being sick, we can determinedly choose our response to be hopeful and 'glass half full'.

Activation

What, if any, effects have you seen in your body from stress or trauma? How have you responded to these?

If you don't love yourself, you won't be happy with yourself. If you can't love yourself, you can't love anyone else.
Kemi Sogunle

DAY ELEVEN

Date

Going Deeper…how what you think affects the rest of you

We're going to spend today looking a bit deeper into the relationship between body and spirit or, put more simply, our mental and physical health, and we're doing this with the help of a cancer specialist named Bernie Siegel who, in a nutshell, treats his patients on the basis that they're going to recover. In his book, Love, Medicine and Miracles, he tells us that,

> *"The fundamental problem most patients face is an inability to love themselves, having been unloved by others during some crucial period of their lives. This period is almost always childhood, when our relationships with our parents establish our characteristic ways of reacting to stress. As adults we repeat these reactions and make ourselves vulnerable to illness, and our personalities often determine the specific nature of the illnesses. The ability to love oneself…enables one to improve the quality of life."*

There's a lot to think about in this one quote. What it's telling us is that the relationship, or lack of it, that we had with our parents, or lack of parents, will have determined what we think of ourselves as adults, and what we think of ourselves as adults will determine every aspect of our attitude towards life and our ability to deal with it in terms of both our physical and mental health. How does that feel?

Before we go any further, remember that in the quote, Bernie is talking about the impact of stress and it's important to understand the inter-relationship between stress and trauma. We've talked about trauma being the outcome of anything that has caused a negative memory to be carried in our brains and the outworking of that memory in our heart. What happens is that how we feel in our hearts influences how we think of ourselves, our self-esteem. And then, the level of our self-esteem will determine how well we cope with life. In turn, how well we cope with life will determine the levels of stress that we carry. Which will then determine how well we respond to sickness or, indeed, whether sickness is provoked within us.

On the face of it, there's a bit of an inevitability about all of this. It sounds as if a traumatic childhood carries no option other than to lead to a lifetime of difficulties, compounded by an increased likelihood to be ill, BUT that's just not the complete story. It ignores how our natural resilience as humans empowers us to overcome life's obstacles. It doesn't allow for how, even in the worst of circumstances, a single kindly act or caring person can change the way things impact us so that we 'manage' and continue to live a 'normal' life. And it certainly doesn't allow for what you're doing now, learning how to hear your heart and chasing your inner healing. What we've been doing so far in each of the days we've been together is learning about ourselves and what makes us what we are. We're about to learn what to do about it!

Thought Stop

Today's message helps to unpack yesterday's 'Thought Stop', hopefully underlining the importance of taking ownership of our life experience so far, understanding what's affected us and how, and determining to do something about it.

Activation

Consider how your thinking has changed since starting on Day One. Can you think of any differences? How would you describe them?

> *Judge not, and you will not be judged; condemn not, and you will not be condemned; forgive, and you will be forgiven.*
>
> Luke 6:37

DAY TWELVE   Date

At Last!...Exploring the healing in forgiveness

For anyone who has already received inner healing of any sort (or body-mind healing as it's sometimes called), what we're about to tell you won't come as a great surprise, because the thing that will most help you to start the journey towards confronting and overcoming the trauma of your past is…forgiveness. Forgiveness is a great healer, it releases emotional pain in a way that just about nothing else can do, and it's free! Or not quite, because when we forgive someone, we have to release a bit of ourselves to them. They may never know you've forgiven them, but you will, and there'll have been a cost, however small, in the doing, but the exchange, what you're 'buying', is so much greater than any cost.

A good description is that, "Forgiveness means letting go of your right to punish or get even," the inference being that in letting go of, releasing yourself from, the right to punish you let go of any resentment, bitterness, anger or hatred that might be there, which won't be the case if you cling to any 'rights'.

Let's clear a misconception. You do not have to physically address the person you're choosing to forgive. You don't have to go up to them, or even email or phone them to forgive them…which is just as well because in the majority of cases they probably don't know the offense, hurt and wounding they have caused you. Perhaps oddly, they don't even need to still be alive. That primary school teacher would be astonished, and probably mortified, at the negative effect they had in their pupil's life. Another thing is, they don't have to deserve your forgiveness, there's no making amends.

So, if we're not actually telling the person they're forgiven, and you're forgiving even though they don't deserve it, then what's the point? It's as we mentioned above, it's for ourselves that we forgive, not for the person we're forgiving. They may also benefit, but primarily it's for us. That's why it doesn't matter if they're still alive, it's the act of giving them the gift of your forgiveness that releases something within you. And it's something we choose to do for ourselves.

Who to forgive? You may have a list of people who you feel have trampled you down over the years and they'll not be a bad place to start, but what you'll find is that the deep healing will come when you start to identify those who caused you the original hurts, those whose actions precipitated the traumas that changed your life. These people may be relatively easy to name if you're thinking of a specific event, but what if your trauma is as the result of a childhood of poverty or parental fighting, of being treated as a slave or just ignored? These are the deep, long-term traumas and, very often, the outworking in our life can be so much a part of us that we find them hard to see, but give it time, and as you begin to heal, you'll see more.

One more point. You may decide that, for instance, your parents couldn't help their behaviour or what they did to you, and maybe that's true in that they were themselves the product of their childhoods and so couldn't help but pass on their own stresses and negative behaviours, but whatever it was it still harmed us and needs to be forgiven for us to be released from it. Perhaps a simple example might help. Let's say again that Dad was never there for you. You therefore grew up feeling abandoned and unloved. The truth is that Dad was in the Army and was away serving his country, which in itself is laudable, but doesn't detract from your feelings. You will still need to forgive him for how what he did made you feel. Going through the process which you'll read about in a couple of days' time will start to help you put the pain of the past behind you.

Thought Stop

Of course, it's quite possible that you might consider forgiveness to be a total waste of time and that, in essence, we should just suck up what people have done to hurt us in the past. If that's you, please stop for a moment and consider. Could it be that the very thought of having to revisit the past is enough to stop you from doing it? Maybe it's like a dark cave that you really don't want to go near? Think of it differently, maybe it's you in the dark cave and the green and bright outside is too scary and unknown to contemplate...and yet people all around you are living out there.

Activation

Go on, try it...think of one person and one thing that you can forgive. Consciously forgive them for what they did, how it made you feel and how it affected your life. How did doing that make you feel now? (Lots of 'feeling', but feelings are good when they're safe!)

The more you know yourself, the more you forgive yourself. It is very easy to forgive others their mistakes; it takes more grit and gumption to forgive them for having witnessed your own. Do as the heavens have done, forget your evil; With them forgive yourself.

Attributed to Shakespeare

DAY THIRTEEN

Date

Emotional Baggage...unpacking the pain of the past

There's another misconception about forgiveness that needs to be dealt with. It's the idea that that in forgiving someone you're condoning what they did. Even worse, that in forgiving them you're inherently re-establishing relationship. Both of these are nonsense. Why would you allow someone who has treated you cruelly back into your life? Why would you ever trust someone who has abused you again? You wouldn't. You don't have to. You're not forgiving to make them feel better, you're forgiving to release yourself from the pain they have caused you.

Just for a moment think of a painful memory. How do you feel about the person who caused you that pain? Is there any resentment or even hatred towards them? Any bitterness? Do you feel angry? Would you like to give them as good as you got? If there is, if you do, then although you may not think about it every day, you're carrying the weight of those negative feelings with you. They may be buried deep but we can guarantee that they, together with all the other hurts and wounds you carry, will be having an effect. To the extent that they colour your responses to life they'll be stealing your joy, and because you've been carrying them for so long you probably won't even know it... until they're dealt with.

We call this 'emotional baggage' and, as we've said, we drag it around with us until it's dealt with. Very often, other people can see it or feel it in us, (remember Emotion I and II?) whilst we remain oblivious. Have you ever known someone who seems to carry the weight of the world on their shoulders? Or someone who is entirely joyless? Or painfully shy, or cannot handle praise, or is overly fearful? It's all as a result of emotional baggage.

What may come as a surprise, until you think about it, is that we are often our own worst critics. It makes sense, really. If others have found fault in us or treated us hurtfully or abused us, something inside us will try and tell us that we probably somehow deserved it. Not all of it, not as bad as it was, but there must have been something there that they responded to. And that must have been our fault. What our brains are doing is trying to rationalise the unacceptable, to make sense of something deeply significant, someone hurting us for no obvious reason, that simply doesn't compute, and, often, the only conceivable answer is, it must be something about us, or something we've done. We blame ourselves.

Often, then, the first person to forgive is ourselves, for having believed what others have said about us. For thinking that we deserved what has happened. That we attracted the attention we got.

Thought Stop

Forgiving ourselves may seem an odd concept but, as we said above, we're often hard on ourselves and our own worst critic. Sometimes it's a step worse than this and, for whatever reason, we feel we deserve whatever comes our way and even invite negative things into our lives as a sort of self-punishment...why? Here's a suggestion, the thing that has happened to us can be so unexpected, uninvited, unjustified and appalling that the only 'reason' that our brains can muster is that it must have been our fault, that there's something bad within us that others can see, and we need to be punished for it. And of course this isn't true.

Activation

Is there anything in your life that you feel you need to forgive yourself for? It doesn't have to be as dramatic as the 'Thought Stop', it can be for mistreating a past relationship or cheating on your taxes. You'll know. The word 'repentance' means 'turning away from' and repenting for things we need to forgive ourselves for is a great way to begin the process.

The heaviest baggage we carry is not in our suitcases, but in our hearts, the weight of unresolved emotions and past experiences.
Unattributed.

DAY FOURTEEN

Date

...and how to deal with it

If we're so oblivious to this emotional baggage we've been talking about, then how can we possibly deal with it? And if the first person we often need to forgive is ourselves, how do we know what to forgive ourselves for? If you don't know the answer, it's in what we suggested right back on Day One. We can ask our hearts. If you didn't try it at the time, ask it now. "Heart, what pain am I carrying?" and then, "Heart, who do I need to forgive for that pain?"

Again, if you've already received inner healing of any sort you've probably been led through similar questions by the person you've been with. Allow us the observation here that inner healing, which is what forgiveness is an element of, is far easier to go through and experience if it's done with someone who knows what they're doing. Those people who have been trained to help others through the process will do so gently, in a way that will help you to forgive those who have caused you trauma, without having to revisit the memories, so it's safe.

Let's get back to asking your heart questions. You may be wondering what you do, having heard who it is you need to forgive for whatever your heart brought your attention to. Here's a structure for your questioning that will keep you on track:

Heart, what pain am I carrying?
Heart, who do I need to forgive for that pain?
Heart, what specifically do I need to forgive them for?
Heart, how did that make me feel?
Heart, what effect did their doing that to me have on my life?

Five questions. The first two set the scene, but why the third? Why 'specifically'? The answer is that you may yourself be surprised at what your heart tells you.

Can you cope with going back to the example of the primary school teacher again? For a moment, stand in the shoes of the adult who had been the little boy or girl made fun of and embarrassed in front of the whole class. Your heart has answered your first two questions, and then you ask that third question, and there's a surprise. Your memory is about the embarrassment, but you heart tells you that specifically you have to forgive the teacher for purposefully picking you out, for drawing attention to you. It's not what you were expecting. And that unexpected answer could unlock the door to a whole area of hurt you maybe knew was there, but you've never fully understood.

Thought Stop

You may think you've already forgiven that person for what they did. You may feel you've forgiven them for how they made you feel too, and so you may be surprised to find that the pain they caused remains. It's normal. You may have to forgive them a hundred times, but each will be for something slightly different, a different hurt on a different day causing hurt again a different way. The good news is that there will be an end to it. One day you'll be left with the memory with no pain or resentment attached to it. We promise.

Activation

Are there people who you feel you've forgiven in the past, but still feel stirred up by when you think of them now? Or hurts you thought you'd left behind that reoccur as dreams or flashbacks? Could you bring them into the open and make a list? If so, it's the start point to dealing with them once and for all. The next few days will give you the opportunity to do so.

My child, if you take my words to heart, and listen for my commandments; if you tune your ear to wisdom and your heart to understanding; if you cry out for understanding, and search for it like it was buried treasure ...then you will understand what it is to be in awe of God, and you will discover what God desires for you.

Proverbs 2: 1-5

DAY FIFTEEN

Date

Going Through Forgiveness…learning to hear from your heart

We're continuing from yesterday. You've asked the question, "Heart, what specifically do I need to forgive that teacher for?" and, to your surprise, the answer hasn't been what you were expecting. It's not for her cruelty or for making fun of you, it's something rather different, it's for deliberately picking you out and drawing attention to you.

Your next question reveals more. "Heart, how did that make me feel?" And the answer comes back, "It made you feel different, like you didn't belong." And here were you thinking all along that 'all' you'd been carrying were feelings of being stupid. And now you've actually, for the first time, asked your heart about it, you discover it's way deeper, that underlying any feelings of being stupid there's a deeper belief, that you didn't belong in the first place, that you're somehow different, that you didn't have the right to be there.

Your final question can reveal even more. "Heart, what effect did their doing that to me have on my life?" This is a question to take slowly, because it could take some time for your heart to unpack the extent of the out-working of these feelings in your life. On Day Six we mentioned cause and effect. What we believe will determine our emotions and the expression of those emotions in feelings. Being made to feel stupid will encourage us to think we are stupid. If we're stupid, why try? because it won't get us anywhere and, as we said earlier, the trickle-down effect of that self-belief will infect every aspect of our lives. But what our heart is showing us now is how the deeper truth of feeling we didn't belong gave being stupid the right to exist. "It's OK being stupid because I don't belong anyway." It's a level of self-justification that may explain how feeling stupid was able to gain such a foothold… and, given time, your heart will unpack it all.

That's where forgiveness starts, and it's a choice. There's something very different between feeling coerced into forgiving someone and doing so because you want to. And there's something very liberating about making that choice in spite of the history. We'll use that poor primary teacher as our example, "I'm choosing to forgive Miss Perkins…"

And then there's the "What for, specifically?" and, as we said above, your heart will have told you exactly what it is that you're choosing to forgive that person for, so add that to your prayer, "I'm choosing to forgive Miss Perkins for purposefully picking me out, for drawing attention to me…"

"Heart, how did that make me feel?", we know the answer, that it made me feel different, like I didn't belong, so we add this, "I'm choosing to forgive Miss Perkins for purposefully picking me out, for drawing attention to me and for making me feel that I didn't belong…"

And then we add what your heart has told you about the effect it had on you. "I'm choosing to forgive Miss Perkins for purposefully picking me out, for drawing attention to me and for making me feel that I didn't belong. I forgive her how I've felt an outsider all my life, how I've felt put up with and an onlooker, that I can't really be a part of anything." And of course, the effects could be both deeper and more damaging.

Taking that hurt, understanding how it made you feel, and what effect it had on your life, and forgiving the person concerned will change everything…but what do you do with it then?

Thought Stop and Activation

Perhaps oddly, todays 'Thought Stop' is 'Don't'! Don't stop and think and try and apply logic, don't decide that none of this makes sense, or that it doesn't work or that it's asking too much or it's too complicated. Please, just go with the flow…hear your heart, trust what it tells you, write it down and keep writing until you're dry. And then ask for more, there may be a well of things and feelings that your heart had been waiting for you to release, and if so, don't stop it, keep writing…

To forgive is to set a prisoner free and discover that the prisoner was you.
Lewis B. Smedes

DAY SIXTEEN

I Choose to Forgive...how to forgive and really mean it

Choosing to forgive someone is massive in itself, especially if it's for something that has caused you life-changing pain. Somehow, though, forgiveness needs to be represented by a physical gesture, something more to show that it's done and there are several ways that people do this. Some people write their forgiveness on a piece of paper, wrap it around a stone and throw it into deep water. In other ministries the hurt is taken and simply dropped in the bin. In the Sozo healing ministry the hurt, once forgiven, is given to Jesus. What's important is that you find completion in whatever you do and then move on to the next thing to be forgiven.
A useful illustration in understanding forgiveness is to think of a bicycle wheel. If there's someone in your life who you feel you have to forgive for many things, think of them as being at the hub of the wheel. Each spoke then represents not so much a different thing you need to forgive them for, an event, but rather the potentially many ways it made you feel and what it made you think or believe about yourself. Turn that wheel just a few degrees and you might find that you need to forgive that same person for the same thing, but maybe for a different outcome, or because you were a year older and how you felt wasn't the same. And that's fine, this isn't a quick fix-it, there's no rush. You're dealing with a lifetime of hurt, releasing it into that deep water or into the bin or to Jesus, item by item.

There's something else you can do to make your forgiveness more direct and personal. You can address the person you're forgiving. Instead of saying, "I choose to forgive Miss Perkins..." you can think of her in your mind's eye and say to her, "Miss Perkins, I'm choosing to forgive you..." Of course, in the natural, you're not speaking to her at all, and for all you know she may be long dead, but somehow speaking directly is very powerful, and, who knows, if you believe in that other dimension we talked about the other day, your forgiveness may be more far reaching than you know.

Lastly, for today, think back to the sequence of questions we suggested you ask your heart. The last one of these was, "Heart, what effect did their doing that to me have on my life?" The answer to this should reveal to you just how what happened, and how it made you feel, changed your approach and interaction with your daily life. There's another equally valid question that you could ask, it's, "Heart, what lie have I believed about myself as a result of the pain inflicted on me?" or "as a result of the trauma I experienced?" or even "as a result of my Dad not being there for me?" Of course, your heart could give you one or more of a myriad answers, but let's assume for a moment that your heart tells you that you believed that you were worthless, then, what we suggest is that you speak out your rejection to that lie, "I reject and renounce the lie that I'm worthless" and then go on to ask your heart the truth, "Heart, what's the truth about that?" and your heart should give you a very different idea about you…not least because no one is worthless, but that's not all…

Thought Stop

These are deep waters, and you may well be astonished and upset by the things about yourself that you've taken as being absolutely a part of who you are and you're now discovering are anything but. There could be a temptation to be hard on yourself as you look back on how what you've believed about yourself has affected your approach to life. Please don't be. All of us have an innate mechanism that causes us to respond to life's challenges by protecting ourselves in any way we have to, even if it's by believing lies about ourselves to keep us 'safe'. Once we recognise these 'protectors' we can, usually with help, call them out and deal with them.

Activation

Can you begin to identify behaviours in your life that you've unconsciously allowed to form part of your identity? Take the worthlessness mentioned above, how would believing that change one's life and direction. Or if you were always told to' shut up' as a child, what lie might you have believed all your life about having opinions and being able to voice them? See if you can think of any negative behaviours you have that you're not happy with, and then ask your heart how you learned them and through whom.

Seek the Lord with all your heart, and you will find Him.
Deuteronomy 4:29, paraphrase

DAY SEVENTEEN

Finding your Higher Power...who really answers those deeper questions?

Perhaps now would be a good time to introduce something that may also not come as a great surprise. Everything we've talked about so far is biblical. The Bible is extraordinarily wise. It's packed with wisdom, and we can learn a great deal from it. It tells us that we are body, soul and spirit, and that we should think of ourselves wholistically, as did Socrates' friend. It speaks of our emotions and feelings and that we should forgive from the heart and, in doing that, it recognises that forgiving from our heads, merely going through the action of forgiving the memory in our brains, achieves very little. If we forgive from our hearts, we can take ownership of our journey from trauma to forgiveness, we can forgive how that event made us feel and the trauma it caused us.

Did you wonder why we said that the person we forgive might also benefit? Have you ever thought about someone and had them contact you within moments? Or had an intuitive feeling about something and, later, wished you'd listened to yourself? Or have you ever prayed? Because if you have then you're admitting a belief that there's more to life than what we can see and sense. It's in that 'other dimension' that those we forgive somehow know that something has changed. Believing in the existence of that 'other dimension' opens the door to many possibilities, not the least 'faith'.

So, today feels like a good time to talk a little more about this 'extra dimension', after all, we've been asking you to ask questions of your heart expecting to hear an answer, so how does that work? Where does that answer come from? And that last question yesterday, about the truth, how about that one?

An easy and perhaps obvious response is that any internal voice that we hear comes from our subconscious and that we answer our own questions based on deep, hidden knowledge and thoughts, our buried responses to life, if you want. So, our heads hold the memories and our hearts our emotional responses, and we can quiz our hearts as to how we feel about our memories and about our feelings. We don't need a higher power to do this, although we might question by what miracle it happens.

Where things get more interesting is when we start to ask questions about the answers we've been giving ourselves. Let's go back a few days to Miss Perkins. You'll remember that we asked our heart what, specifically, we needed to forgive her for, how it made us feel and what affect her doing what she did had on us and our life from that moment. There's more we can do though, because we can add further questions. "What lies have I believed about myself as a result of Miss Perkins?" would be one. And then one that's at the centre of our thought today, "What's the truth?"

Arguably the answer to, "What lies have I believed about myself as a result of Miss Perkins?" can also come from our own innate comprehension of life and deep well of experience, but the same cannot be said for the answer to "What's the truth?" That's a question that we cannot answer for ourselves. It can only be answered by a 'third party' who knows you, all about you and everything surrounding you. And my suggestion is that that's God. And now you have a choice. You can either reject that idea out of hand, or you can accept it and test it. If you're determined that God is either non-existent or not for you then you might want to skip to Day Twenty-One, but I hope you won't!

How do you test the existence or presence of God? How about asking Him some of those questions you may have been storing up for such an occasion, questions such as, "God, what do you think of me?" "God, what do I think of you?" "God, what do I think of me?" "God, what lies do I believe about you?" and then, again, "God, what's the truth?" Expect to hear an answer and accept the very first thing you hear, see, sense or feel, because that will be God. The second thing will be you thinking about it! Over time you will grow to recognise the difference between your own voice and His. All of which may well read as a very glib way of explaining what should be a deep and very meaningful revelation, that our creator, God Almighty, cares enough for each one of us to want to communicate with us, and that He's just waiting for us to let Him. Everything in the Christian faith points towards this one truth; God is love. Jesus was all about being a pointer to His Father's nature, and His message to us can be distilled down to 'love God, love your neighbour'. Following Jesus is only about love, and relationship is the truest expression of love. I'm rubbing it in, but isn't listening and responding to each other, and God, in love the truest expression of love itself? Wouldn't God want to have a working two-way relationship with those He loves and calls His children? I rest my case... until tomorrow!

Thought Stop

Those who most rebel against the idea of there being a 'God' are often those who feel most let down and disappointed by Him. And sometimes that disappointment is so great that we don't give Him a second chance. Please don't let that be you.

Activation

How is your relationship with God? Have you even given it any thought recently? In the best of all worlds, how would you like it to be? We'll be looking closer at this tomorrow.

Once we learn to pray with our hearts, and not our lips, we truly begin to have a conversation with God.

Unknown

DAY EIGHTEEN

Date

Why Would He Bother?...a challenge for the truth

Over the last few days you've been taken through a process of forgiveness that has involved asking your heart questions. No matter what your faith position has been, we hope you've gone along with the process and that it's made sense to you. We've also sprung on you the thought that God wants to be in relationship with each and every one of us and that we can ask Him questions and expect to hear an answer, and we've suggested that even if you're sceptical about the existence of God you give Him the opportunity to prove He's there.

It may or may not surprise you to read that in our experience the majority of the Christians we've worked with over the years do not have a personal two-way relationship with God, two-way meaning that when they pray to Him they hear or see or sense of feel a response. Most Christians do a lot of asking for things in their prayers, not so many then stop to listen to what He has to say. When you think about it, it's an odd idea to speak out prayers, expecting them to be heard, and then not to wait for a reply. If you were asking a friend to do something for you, we assume you'd wait to see what they said. It just makes sense.

Most of what we do then, in our time with people is help them to hear from God for themselves, so, if you're a Christian or not, the good news is that a relationship, a friendship with God is just waiting to happen. As a non-Christian you may read this and still think yourself excluded. You're not. There aren't any pre-qualifications to having a relationship with God, any more than there are in forming a friendship with anyone else. You just have to be willing.

How are you doing with this? If the idea of God remains a bit challenging then try this. You'll almost certainly have heard of Alcoholics Anonymous or Narcotics Anonymous and their 12 Step Programmes. It's widely used in one form or another in alcohol and substance abuse recovery and it depends on a belief in a 'higher power', a something that is greater than us. For many, God is that higher power. For others, a higher power isn't associated with religion or a deity, it's a connection that we share with all living things. Some people don't try to understand their higher power. They believe humans can't comprehend it, and again some others believe that we're all here courtesy of a cosmic co-incidence. And that's fine…even so, here's my challenge to you, have you ever sat down and really sorted out your thoughts as to what you believe? Have you perhaps discarded faith in God in the absence of evidence? Your answer will place you in one of three camps, you'll either believe in a 'higher power' or not, or you'll be open to persuasion!

Today, spend some time thinking about this and working out what you believe and why. If your inclination is to reject the idea of God as a 'higher power' we challenge you to really look at this and to, at least, accept the possibility…or wait until you've read tomorrow's thought!

Thought Stop and Activation

If your inclination is to reject the idea of God why not have a look at:

https://www.premierunbelievable.com/articles/a-most-reluctant-convert-why-guillaume-bignons-story-is-powerful-evidence-for-god/13487.article

and see what you think? Whatever your view, it's an interesting watch!

But you, O Lord, are a God of compassion and mercy, slow to get angry and filled with unfailing love and faithfulness.
Psalm 86:15

DAY NINETEEN

Date

A Relationship of Love…discovering God's love for you

Why this harping on about faith and God?

Well it's hard for us to talk about baggage, inner-healing and forgiveness without referring to faith, you'll probably have picked that up by now. You don't have to have a faith in anything, but the truth is that it's much harder to find healing and wholeness on your own. We ended the other day reflecting on what amounts to the essence of the Christian faith, that God loves us and wants to share our life, and that, therefore, life is all about relationship and our relationship with Him should be a two-way conversation that shifts the burden of having to be strong in ourselves and totally self-reliant, to a life of sharing all the bad things in life with a heavenly Father who is, after all, the ultimate healer. Being able to share life's hurts makes all the difference.

Think of it like this: we can tell you here and now and as a fact that God loves you and thinks you're wonderful, because that's His promise. We can also tell you that your trespasses, the things you know you've done wrong, can be forgiven (and therefore what other people have done wrong too). But that's just us telling you, and repeating Day Five! Whether you have faith or not you'll probably read on from that last sentence without receiving much impact from it. You may even have to read back to see what it said, which, to save you doing so, was that "God loves you and thinks you're wonderful, because that's His promise. We can also tell you that your trespasses, the things you know you've done wrong, can be forgiven (and therefore what other people have done wrong too)". If you've read that sentence, twice now, without it impacting you, don't feel too bad, because that's the usual response. They're just words on the page. They're just head knowledge, if that.
BUT, if, on the other hand, you were to hear those words from God himself, or from Jesus, the son He sent to earth to lead us to Him, that He

loves you and thinks you're wonderful, and that all your sins can be forgiven, that would hopefully have a rather deeper impact. That's the beauty of knowing and having a two-way relationship with your creator, the one who made you. And you can do that. And you don't have to profess Christianity, or any other belief for it to happen. After all, if you had to be a Christian before you could hear from Him, how would anyone hear His call and decide to follow Him?

Thought Stop and Activation

How many people do you know? How many are friends? How many do you share your deepest secrets with? How many do you trust? How many can you rely on to help you in an hour of need? If you're like most of us, the answer is, not many…why not make a list and for each name spend some time thinking just how deep your relationship goes. This isn't to make you feel isolated or alone, but it is to contrast human friendships with the deep and personal relationship we can have with our creator.

So do not fear, for I am with you; do not be dismayed, for I am your God.
Isaiah 41:10

When I am afraid, I put my trust in you. In God, whose word I praise, in God I trust; I shall not be afraid.
Psalm 56:3-4

DAY TWENTY

Date

Why Choose God?...can God really be trusted?

There's a very deep and confusing rub to the conversation about accepting the possibility of God and, roughly speaking, it runs along the lines of "If God exists, why does He allow pain and poverty and suffering and disasters? How can I believe in a God like that?" It's a very valid point. There's an excellent and easily digested short booklet called 'Why Does God Allow Suffering?' by Nicky Gumbel (the chap behind the Alpha Course, www.alpha.org) that goes a long way to giving palatable answers to these thorniest of questions. In it Nicky says:

One, that God has given man choice and that, when you look into the history behind almost all the bad things that happen, it's as a result of man's bad choices. Why did He give us choice? Because He loves us. If He was a dictator, would we think to love Him?

Two, God allows suffering because He works through it. On the face of it this sounds challenging, if not nonsense, but think about it. Who needs God when everything is rosy in our lives? Most of us turn to God in times of trouble. And, back to point one, so much of suffering is as a result of other people, and our own, bad choices.

Three, that experience shows that God compensates us in and for our suffering, however caused.

Four, that in what happened to Jesus, God's son on Earth, He, God, has shared in and understands our suffering.

Is that it? Is that all we need to know to overcome all the objections one could have against believing in and having faith in God? No. Not a bit of it. Hopefully it's enough to crack open that door of doubt. It's an odd thing, but once you allow the possibility of God being true to enter your being He usually grabs the opportunity. It's then up to you to develop the relationship by asking Him things and expecting to hear an answer.

U2's Bono puts it exceptionally well in his biography 'Surrender' when talking about his bandmate, Adam Clayton's journey to knowing God: "It's an extraordinary thing," writes Bono, "the moment of surrender. To get down on your knees and ask the silence to save you, to reveal itself to you. To kneel down, to implore, to throw yourself out into space, to quietly whisper or roar your insignificance. To fall prostate and ask to be carried. To humble yourself with your family, your band mates, and to discover if there's a face or name to that silence."

Even the most 'Christian' of Christians experience times when they have doubts about God's existence and love. Finding faith and then holding it is a lifetime's journey, but it's one built on relationship and a very good place to start is hearing God as He answers your questions.

Thought Stop

Very few of us are completely without an opinion about God. Most of us who don't believe in Him or simply reject Him do so out of hurt or disappointment. At some point He simply wasn't there when He was needed, or He didn't come through, much as we prayed. And there's no easy answer to this, it's a conundrum that all who believe in God have to struggle with. One way through is to look at the amazing miracles and stories of complete turn-around in people's lives, in other words at things He has done, rather than at things He hasn't. If we knew all the answers we wouldn't need faith.

Activation

Think of some of the disappointments in your life. Did things work out in spite of them? Then think of some of the good things that have happened, the blessings you've received, do you believe they were all due to coincidence? Do you notice a thread of any sort running through your life?

I pray with great faith for you, because I'm fully convinced that the One who began this glorious work in you will faithfully continue the process of maturing you and will put his finishing touches to it until the unveiling of our Lord Jesus Christ!

Philippians 1:6 TPT version

DAY TWENTY-ONE   Date

What's the Point?...where is all this taking me?

We're starting our final full week of this walk together, so let's have another quick recap. Our journey started with gaining an understanding of how important our emotions and feelings are to us and how we can learn to understand and engage with both of these. We learned how our own truths may not always reflect what was actually going on and how our own understanding of those truths will have shaped our lives, especially if we've experienced trauma. We then looked at the effects that the experience of trauma can have on us, and that being able to forgive the perpetrators of those traumas is a key to receiving freedom from what their effects are doing in our lives. The next few days were spent learning how to forgive, of learning how to relate to one's heart as part of the forgiveness journey. And then came the question, if we're now able to hear from our hearts, where do your heart answers come from? That lead to a conversation about finding your higher power, all of which brings us to today and, to put it bluntly, what's the point? Where is all this taking me?

It's a valid question and it's one that applies to any inner-healing counselling or ministry, or indeed to any self-discovery course or self-help book. We don't all, but we should all, have a desire to better ourselves, to be the best version of ourselves. Now you may have this desire slightly selfishly, because you want to maybe be successful and make more money, or unselfishly, because the best version of you is good for your family and society as a whole but either way, having the intention is an acknowledgment that none of us are everything we could be...or in Christian terms, none of us are everything that God made us to be. All of us can be better people, whatever 'being better' means to you. Once we accept this, our journey towards that end can begin.

Personal betterment can take many forms, but the word one usually hears being bandied about in conversations about self-improvement is authenticity. When the Harvard Business Review surveyed the employees of thousands of businesses to find what they considered to be the most important quality in a boss, the top by far was authenticity. And authenticity, as with respect or honour, is not something you can claim for yourself, it's something others see in you. Authenticity is being comfortable in your skin, knowing where you come from and who you are, no matter what company you are in or the circumstances you're experiencing. If you're a Jesus follower it's about knowing who you are and whose. You could say that authenticity is the goal that self-discovery and inner healing should take us to. There are many definitions of authenticity but one that cuts to the chase is that being authentic means staying true to who you are, what you do and who you think of yourself as doing everything for, and that's what we'll look at over the next few days.

Thought Stop

Do you live your life purely for your own benefit or to add to and improve the life of those around us? It's maybe a deeper question than it first appears. Even the most self-centred amongst us inevitably adds to or detracts from the life of more than just ourselves, like it or not. All of us play a role in the lives around us, as an employee, workmate, family member or even as a tenant or bus passenger; any interaction with others contributes to or detracts from them, for good or bad. Our attitude will largely be determined by how we see ourselves and then the use we consider ourselves to be to others.

Activation

Think of the people you inter-relate with, those whose life you touch as a part of your own. How would they see you and think of you? How would you like them to see and think of you? Is it as the true you, or the someone you're seen as being because of life's circumstances? What would it take for you to be the person you'd like to be seen as, in all your relationships?

> *We often do not realize how blind we are. We often do evil, and we do worse in excusing ourselves. We rebuke small faults in others but overlook greater faults in ourselves. We are too quick to resent and feel what we suffer from others but fail to consider how much others suffer from us.*

Thomas à Kempis

DAY TWENTY-TWO   Date

Simply You…finding who we're meant to be

In his book, 'The Gift of Being Yourself' David Benner tells us that, "Simple being is tremendously difficult to achieve and fully authentic being is extremely rare." At first glance one could think there's a typo here, surely it's meant to read 'simply being", but no, it's 'simple being' and it's contrasted with 'fully authentic being', so what do they both mean?

One thing 'simple being' does not mean is anything to do with being mentally challenged. What it does mean, on the other hand, is to be someone who can find happiness in the smallest things, who is content with what they have, and who finds ways to make space for what matters most to them, letting go of the rest. It's living life being true to yourself. Timothy was right when he wrote, "Godliness with contentment is great gain."(1 Tim 6:6)

How do we do that, and isn't it naïve to think that we can live like that in the midst of everything that's happening in life? Won't we just be pushed around by circumstances?

The answer is 'no', not if your 'simple being' is premised on the second part of that Benner quote of being 'a fully authentic being'. Yesterday's definition of authenticity helps us to clarify, 'staying true to who you are and what you do and who you think you're doing everything for'. If we are capable of meeting this definition then we're certainly capable of 'simple living', in fact the one almost automatically leads out of the other; remember, authenticity is the goal from which true life can flow, it's what we believe leads to contentment.

If, then, authenticity is knowing who we are truly meant to be (and whose, for Jesus-followers), then how do we become that person? What's our start point? The thing here is that until we know who we are, what we stand for, how we respond to things, what we believe and why we are what we are, good, bad, indifferent and ugly, we cannot begin the journey towards authenticity. In short, what is our identity (who we feel we are on the inside), and how would an authentic version of me differ from the me I am now?

Introducing the idea of identity brings with it other questions. So many of us identify more with what we do than who we are. Are you a sales manager or business leader more than you are a wife or brother? Does being able to say that you're a doctor, shop assistant or road worker give you a title or position to hide the rest of you behind? And then, what is there about the rest of you that you're not happy to promote as who you are? Is it because you feel the need to prove yourself through your vocation or job, or is it because you're not happy with or even maybe ashamed of what you feel you really are? And why is that?

If these questions appear harsh, we're sorry, they're meant to provoke rather than chastise. Authenticity demands that we bring every aspect of our present identity into the light for us to look at and then decide whether this bit of us is something we'd be happy for everyone to see and know, or not, and it can be a painful process. That's discovering the 'what'. Discovering the 'why' of what we are inevitably takes us back to our main subject, facing and healing the pain of the past carried in our heart. And hopefully, now we can hear from our heart and ask it (and our creator) questions, that has become possible

Thought Stop

Proverbs 23:7 of the Bible tells us that "As a man thinketh in his heart, so he is." It suggests that our thoughts shape our reality, and that by changing the way we think, we can change the way we experience the world and how the world interacts with us. One way to put these quotes into practice is by being present and observing our thoughts, rather than being caught up in them. Here's a question to consider; how much of what we think of ourselves is done in the light of self-justification? In other words, how many of the negative ways we respond to life do we excuse ourselves for? We tend to defend our thoughts, responses and actions to ourselves, not least because the option is self-condemnation, and that's not acceptable. Authenticity, though, demands that we question our responses to life. Healing demands that we question those responses.

Activation

In the early 1400s, Thomas à Kempis wrote this about knowing ourselves: " We often do not realize how blind we are. We often do evil, and we do worse in excusing ourselves. We rebuke small faults in others but overlook greater faults in ourselves. We are too quick to resent and feel what we suffer from others but fail to consider how much others suffer from us." How does it feel to read this?

Even things about yourself that you most want to change must first be accepted, even embraced. Self-transformation is always preceded by self-acceptance. And the self that you must accept is the self you actually and truly are.

David Benner

DAY TWENTY-THREE

'Positives' and 'Negatives'…learning to be true to yourself

Yesterday's last paragraph told us that the journey to authenticity begins with us admitting to every element of what makes us what and who we are, like it or not. I might like to think of myself as being loving, loyal and a good team player, but I find it less easy or acceptable to think of myself as short tempered, arrogant, prone to white lies…or whatever your particular foibles and failings happen to be. Here's the thing, one isn't somehow truer than the other, though we might like them to be so, they're both true and none of us can change from being anything other than that mix of good and bad until we're willing to embrace them both. David Benner tells us that, "Even things about yourself that you most want to change must first be accepted, even embraced. Self-transformation is always preceded by self-acceptance. And the self that you must accept is the self you actually and truly are."

In case you're reading this and thinking that the 'positive' bits of you outweigh the 'negative' bits or indeed you're thinking that your negative bits are so insignificant that you can safely keep them buried where they only pop up now and again, maybe under stress or when the occasion demands, it's worth noting that it's those things about us that we refuse to acknowledge, or bury deep, that are given increased power and influence by our failure to accept them. It is that which we avoid that will most tyrannise us. He goes on to tell us that, "Self-acceptance does not increase the power of things that ultimately need to be eliminated. Rather, it weakens them. It does so because it robs them of the power that they develop when they operate outside of awareness and outside the embrace of self-acceptance."

Authenticity, then, demands that we be prepared to accept that we're not really as 'good' or 'positive' as we like to think we are and then prepared to do something about it. Otherwise, as Richard Rohr has said, we'll continue to live in bondage to a false self that is not the truly authentic us.

Admitting we have 'negative' bits within us is one thing, identifying them all is another. I may recognise that I'm arrogant and short tempered, but what else is there hiding within me that needs to be winkled out? How do I identify my 'bads'?

Try this! Recognise those things that makes you touchy. If someone tells you to loosen up and it annoys you, well maybe you're taking life too seriously. Or if you feel yourself avoiding the purchase of the next round of drinks, are you being stingy? Do you feel someone is being critical of you? Is self-pride then kicking in? I hope you see the point of this! Negative behaviours stop us from being who we're meant to be, our truly authentic selves.

Thought Stop

There's no blame in all of this and nor should there be shame. We'll look at this tomorrow, but for the moment let this really sink in, those negative bits we're referring to aren't there because we chose them, they're there because of what has happened to us. This doesn't excuse them; it simply explains them. Our mindset needs to be that whatever emotional baggage we carry isn't ours to keep, it's been dumped on us and it's time we got rid of it. As Bernie Siegel says, "We should see ourselves as being perfectly imperfect and accept ourselves that way. I'm not OK, you're not OK and that's OK".

Activation

Bernie Siegel also tells us, "An unreserved positive self-adoration remains the essence of health. Self-esteem and self-love are not sinful." We agree… to a point! What Bernie is talking about here is healthy self-respect, not narcissistic self-adulation!

How does reading this make you feel?

A failure is not always a mistake, it may simply be the best one can do under the circumstances. The real mistake is to stop trying.

BF Skinner

DAY TWENTY-FOUR

Date

The Benefit of Happiness...where do you sit on the 'happy scale'?

Being fully exposed can be uncomfortable. There are those amongst us who can look at our naked selves in a mirror and feel OK about it, and others of us who shudder at the thought. Authenticity is being happy with what you know about yourself and see, and happy for others to see you too...at which point I'll draw that corollary to a close!

So, what next? Let's return to what we've identified as the 'negative' bits, those things inside us we're not proud of. We mentioned a few, self-pride and stinginess for example, but there are so many, and here's an important point, if we carry something negative within us then it's somehow either been planted by something or someone outside of us, or we have allowed something or someone to influence us negatively and we've 'chosen' for whatever reason to accept it...and that's usually due to someone or something having influenced us negatively at some point earlier in our life. How, then, do we deal with these 'negative' bits?

On Day Six we introduced the idea that our hearts hold our perceptions of the truth of events and feelings, good and bad, and on Day Sixteen we ended with forgiving the unfortunate Miss Perkins for picking us out and making us feel we didn't belong (you may have to go back to refresh yourself on the Miss Perkins saga so far!)
And here's today's starter question: would everyone have responded in the same way to being treated badly by her? Would everybody's heart have held the same 'truth' of who we are and therefore responded the same way? Don't worry, it's a rhetorical question and the answer is, no they wouldn't.

One of the keys in most inner healing models is to be able to get to the root of how and when a negative behaviour or limiting self-belief got accepted and embedded into someone's life. It's also something we have to be very careful about doing with someone else. Here's why; much of the negativity in our life is as a result of a trauma and what one never wants to do is cause someone to revisit the memory of a trauma they experienced, usually as a child. Doing so can create such an overwhelming emotional response that they can see and believe themselves to be back in the trauma at the time that it happened, which can be very frightening for them, and for you if you've provoked the memory. Now, though, we're working on the basis that we're asking our own heart questions, but we wanted to flag this up, just in case. This aside, the point is that the way we responded to Miss Perkins attitude and words towards us will have been determined by something that happened to us much earlier in our life. We respond to life out of life experiences (we broached this subject on Day Eleven).

It's a deeply sad observation that depressingly few of us have enjoyed the benefits of growing up in a happy and stable family home with two parents who loved, protected and supplied for us. Instead, an ever-growing number of us have been raised in relatively dysfunctional families, where there were different tensions, behaviours and unhappiness for us to deal with. Each and all of these will have had an effect. For a moment think of a baby born as a result of loving parents after a happy pregnancy and give that baby a score of 100. Now begin to knock off points for any harsh words, threats, deprivations, unkind actions and any other negative things you can think of that potentially can happen to a baby, it doesn't take long for your 100 to be wiped out. And that's before considering any stress or rejection the baby's mother, and baby, may have experienced during pregnancy, factors that may have taken baby's potential score to well below 100, even at birth.

Let's now return to the baby born of happy, contented and loving parents. That baby will be loved, cherished, encouraged and supported through childhood, each kind word, encouragement and praise adding numbers to that 100-point score. Sure, there may be some nastiness at school or a falling out with friends or even worse, but for a child with lots of points in their bag, such things will be far easier to deal with than for our less fortunate baby.

Where does that leave us? Anything said by Miss Perkins to our high scoring baby would quite probably have been shrugged off. For our low scorer, her words would have been another twist of the knife.

Thought Stop and Activation

Where do you think you sit on the points' scale? Try and be brutally honest with yourself, accepting that negative events invariably have had negative consequences. Don't make excuses for anyone or anything. Why things happened doesn't matter, nor does the intention of the people involved; what happened and the effect on you does. What would things have been like if life had taken a kinder path? What do you think you'd have been like?

Whoever heeds discipline shows the way to life, but whoever ignores correction leads others astray.
Proverbs 10;17

DAY TWENTY-FIVE

Date

Going Back to Roots…the behaviours we've carried from childhood

The idea that the root cause for those 'negative' bits we carry originated in our childhood won't come as a great surprise to anyone who's thought about it. The severity and implication of what happened might. Today we're going to start to look at a series of negative behaviours, feelings and emotions that we can be carrying as a result of what happened to us back then. Note that these aren't in any particular order and, hopefully, not all of them will apply! Remember too that whilst these may be things we believe about ourselves, they absolutely need not be true! Also that in the main these traumas are not one-off incidences, a trauma can, and often is, a long and painful exposure to a challenging and debilitating environment.

The classic is low self-esteem, self-worth or of feeling we're just not good enough. If no-one affirmed us and told us we were wonderful as a child, or, worse, if we were ignored and told we were a waste of space, this will be us.

If we have a fear of being abandoned, no matter how much affection or love we are receiving now, that will have a negative impact on the relationships that we're in. Our friends and partners will be constantly having to humour and reassure us, which itself will cause pressures between you.

If we have a problem expressing our true emotions, or even feeling emotions, it could well be because emotions aren't safe things to have, so we've buried them somewhere deep where they can't hurt us.

If we feel the need to say and do the right thing all the time so that everyone is pleased with us it could be because this was the only way we used to be able to get affirmation of any sort. Many of us enjoy pleasing people, it makes us feel good, but being a people pleaser is a different thing altogether. We should be liked for who we are, not what we do.

In the same sort of a way, perfectionism is usually driven by a desire for approval or a fear of criticism, often because acceptance as a child was conditional. This is very much like feeling that one has to perform well to be included or accepted.

Similar to people pleasing is having difficulty in setting boundaries. You may wonder what the similarity is and it's that it has the same root, with that root outworking in very different ways. We should all have friends and family who we would go out of our way to help, others we would help if we can and others again who we would tend not to help unless it was urgent. The problem is when we allow any of these to impose on us to a point beyond our own ability or comfort. Not being able to say "No" is often the result of needing the affirmation and perceived acceptance that comes with saying "Yes". Again, we should be liked for who we are, not what we do. Just one more today, it's self-sabotage. Have you ever felt un-worthy of being given a gift, or being invited to a party or a job you've been offered? Or of being loved? Have you felt so strongly about it that you've turned away or refused? That's self-sabotage. Think of it like this. If a child has been made to feel unwanted and unloved, it may well end up feeling not good enough and deserving of nothing. Such a child could well grow up determined to fail at all things because they're worthless, or even to do so to punish the world by depriving it of all they could have done. It's a very deep and dark place, and it could well have its root in one event that became the final straw.

Thought Stop and Activation

How does going through this list change your point scale from yesterday's Thought Stop and Activation? Does it make you feel any different about your childhood? If so, in what way? What is your emotional response?

But if we freely admit that we have sinned, we find God utterly reliable and straightforward—he forgives our sins and makes us thoroughly clean from all that is evil.

1 John 1:9 Philips.

DAY TWENTY-SIX

Date

Just a Few More…the problem with guilt or shame

We'll start this second day of identifying some of the 'negative' behaviours (or feelings or emotions) we might carry that stop us from being our truly authentic self with this, shame and guilt. We can, of course, carry both guilt and shame for things we've done, or are doing, that we don't feel happy or proud about. We mentioned this a couple of days ago, but it's an important point that bears repetition. If that's you, there's something very important to remember, which is that no matter how heinous the thing you've done, there's an underlying, a root, reason why you've done it and recognising and pulling that root out will help you beat the behaviour.

Many people, though, carry shame and guilt for something that's been done to them, counter-intuitive though this may be. Sometimes what has happened is so appalling that the mind can just not compute or rationalise what has happened and the only explanation that can make any sense at all is that somehow we brought this all on ourself, I attracted this trouble and it's my fault. I have to carry the shame and the guilt that goes with it. And you have to believe it when I tell you that this is just not true in any circumstance. Never feel guilty for something done to you! Never carry shame for someone else's actions!

Having read about guilt and shame it will be no surprise to see negative self-talk on this list. If we have believed any of the things on this list to be 'us' then it's a short step to becoming our own inner critic, thinking we can do nothing right, that we look ugly or/and that we're ugly, stupid and unworthy. This will be especially true if our parents, or those influential adults in our childhood, also told us we couldn't do anything right, were ugly, stupid, unworthy, or worse.

Much in the same vein as both guilt and shame and negative self-talk, but important to mention, is lack of self-compassion. Being able to give oneself a break, to allow oneself some leeway and to not judge oneself harshly is a vital element of an authentic life. The truth is we all make mistakes, we all fail at things, we could all do better, be kinder, love more…but sometimes we don't and that's OK. If it isn't then we are placing impossible demands for perfection on ourselves, maybe considering ourself to be unworthy of anything other than condemnation...and I think that, by now, we'll know where that started in our life.

And there are, obviously, more. A difficulty in intimate relationships would be one and feeling an outsider to life another and each and every one of these has that same root of receiving insufficient love, care, affirmation and provision in childhood.

Where does this list and all the soul searching and self-identification that goes with it lead us to? Hopefully to the point of recognising how far we are from being the fully authentic real us that we're meant to be. And the good news is that we're now fully equipped to do something about it! We'll start tomorrow!

Thought Stop

You'll either recognise yourself in what we've covered in these last two days, or not. Obvious though this sounds, it's an important distinction. On the one hand you may feel a sense of relief in not recognising yourself, on the other a sense of condemnation if you do. We suggest you turn this on its head. All of us, without exception, carry trauma, all of us have behaviours and ways of looking at and doing life that are the result of something that shouldn't have happened. Recognition is the first step towards overcoming and recovery. If you haven't recognised yourself at all, try again! If you have, there is no condemnation, well done!

Activation

What happened? Tomorrow we'll begin to look at some of the 'should-haves' in our life. Today, though, just reflect on the circumstances of your upbringing that may have brought about some of the behaviours (or feelings or emotions) you've identified.

Family is not an important thing, it's everything.
Michael J. Fox

DAY TWENTY-SEVEN

Date

Bringing it all Back Home (Part One)... understanding the impact of family

It's astonishing how we can go through life believing lies about ourselves and thinking it's quite normal. It's deeply sad that so many of us grow up in circumstances that encourage us to do so. And it's tragic that this is something that is increasingly the norm.

How so? Well, we've identified that most of the lies we believe about ourselves stem from our childhood, and on Day Twenty-Four we saw how those brought up in two-parent secure and loving environments seem to get a better deal from life, so let's look more closely at this.

Any way you look at it, our Dads have three important jobs in our lives. They're meant to protect us, so we're not just kept safe but know we're worth keeping safe; they're meant to provide for us, so we don't lack and know we're provided for in love; they're meant to help us form our identity, so that we know who we are and can stand proud and certain. 'Dad' may be Granddad, or Step-Dad or some other authority figure, it can even, to some level, be Mum, but then she has her own job to do. If Dad isn't around to be Dad, or he can't or doesn't know how to (perhaps because of his own father), then there's no role model to learn from and be shaped into manhood by.

Mums comfort us. They impart the basics to us as babies and young children. They're the beating heart we lived with for the first nine months of our existence and the love we (should) feel from them as they hold us means everything. It's rare for there to have been no Mum, and very tough on a child if that's the case. It's not so rare for our Mums not to have wanted us and even resented us being inside of them...and we'll have felt that resentment even before we were born.

Oddly, maybe, our brothers and sisters and the friends we have as children are very important too. We learn who we are from bouncing off them.

They reflect to us how they see us and we adjust accordingly, mostly without knowing we're doing it. If they are genuinely good friends then we will learn and like to be like them, but if they're rough no-goods, that's what we'll accept as being normal and admirable.

Which leaves us where? Hopefully with a growing awareness of what was happening or missing from our life that allowed us to believe that we're all the negative things that we do. Hopefully, in a place where we can start to ask our hearts what lies we believe about ourselves and who we need to forgive for having ever allowed those lies to take root in our hearts. Hopefully, to put into practise what we learned on Day Fifteen about asking our hearts questions and expecting to hear an answer. Hopefully, too, you'll have decided to position yourself so you can hear when you reject the lies and ask for the truth...

Thought Stop

Everything stems back to our parents. Or lack of them. But then their lives were shaped by their parents, and so it goes on through the generations. You may well have to forgive your grandparents for how what they did to your parents in turn affected you. Understanding how cause and effect has worked in your life and in your family line is a major step in breaking the pattern. You don't have to repeat it, it's your choice.

Activation

How much of the 'negative stuff' in your life do you recognise as being something you saw in your parents and maybe learned from them without necessarily meaning to? And then, how much of the good in you do you recognise in them? Make a list of both.

> *You can't heal what you can't feel.*
> John Bradshaw

DAY TWENTY-EIGHT   Date

Bringing it all Back Home (Part Two)… understanding the impact of environment

Yesterday we looked at our parents and siblings and how their attitude and behaviour was responsible for forming so much of our self-belief and relationship with life. Today we're going to have a look at things from a slightly different angle.

We've already said that trauma doesn't have to be caused purely by something or somethings that happen to us as an event (Day Eight), lasting trauma can be caused just by having lived in a traumatic environment, and this to the extent that trauma becomes our normal and we seek trauma or to create traumatic situations because they represent what we grew up with. Let us explain this with the help of Dr Nicole LePera, and begin by telling you that our brains reach 90% of its adult size by the time we're six and continues to develop how it operates until our mid-twenties. Every action and behavioural pattern we experienced in childhood will have impacted our developing nervous system. How our parents and other influential figures interacted with us, handled stress and coped with the upsets in their lives will have been absorbed by our brains as being 'normal'. We will subconsciously seek to emulate this behaviour in our own relationships as adults, usually to our detriment. Over-reaction and shouting may well be our normal.

If, on the other hand, you're a 100 point child (Day Twenty-Four) having enjoyed a stable childhood, you'll tend towards calm and be able to deal with stress quickly, returning to what is called homeostasis, our body's preferred state of balance. In a nutshell, if we kicked and screamed as kids we'll likely kick and scream as adults; if we dealt with pain by drifting off into our own world then, we'll probably react the same way now.

Why does this matter? To be our authentic self we have to recognise how much of the way we respond to life and relationships is governed by conditioning and how much that conditioning has robbed us of the ability to be the people we were meant to be before all the negative stuff happened. Not just that, living with chronic stress, which is what we're talking about here, is extremely bad for our health, each activation releasing the fight / flight / freeze stress chemicals such as cortisol, dopamine, endorphins and adrenaline. You'll probably have heard of people who are 'adrenaline junkies', they're those who are always chasing the next thrill and they are, as the name suggests, addicted to the rush. Those brought up in homes with chaos and unpredictability will similarly have an emotional addiction to that way of life and seek to recreate it as adults. We'll look for arguments, we'll create fallings-out, we'll be victims.

And we don't need to be, because once we recognise what's going on inside us, we can do something about it, and we're back to asking our hearts what lies we're believing about ourselves and who we need to forgive for having created the circumstances for those lies to exist. More importantly we can ask our hearts what the truth of any situation is and start the process of accepting this truth as our new normal, our true and authentic self.

Thought Stop and Activation

How do you feel having read the above? What does homeostasis look like for you? How much would you like your life to be different?

Spirituality emerged as a fundamental guidepost in Wholeheartedness. Not religiosity but the deeply held belief that we are inextricably connected to one another by a force greater than ourselves--a force grounded in love and compassion. For some of us that's God, for others it's nature, art, or even human soulfulness. I believe that owning our worthiness is the act of acknowledging that we are sacred. Perhaps embracing vulnerability and overcoming numbing is ultimately about the care and feeding of our spirits.

Brené Brown

DAY TWENTY-NINE

It's All About Balance…how to be at peace with yourself

Yesterday's 'Thought Stop' question deserves more attention. Homeostasis is, as mentioned, our body's preferred state of balance, it's that place of being at which our body, soul and sprit are at their resonant best, at peace with themselves. We'd also suggest that it's the place where we are best able to explore what true authenticity looks and feels like for ourselves, exploring and establishing who we are and who we are meant to be, and responding to life out of that certainty.

There's a considerable liberation in being free of baggage, free of all the lies we've believed about ourselves, free of fear, free of resentments and the protective need to judge others; free having forgiven all the people who have caused hurt in our life; who could or should have protected us… it should feel like a weight has slipped from your shoulders. Hopefully you're also increasingly free of all those automatic emotional responses, those behaviours that we learned as coping mechanisms when we were young and remained with us as our inner child.

You now know, or at least have a better idea of the 'you' you should be, as you were always made and intended to be. Sure, there'll be steps backwards, there'll be things that happen that act as reminders or cause you pain, but they'll be blips and you'll be able to ask your heart what lie you believed as a result of that 'blast from the past', deal with the lie and return to your homeostasis…

Then what? What could the future hold? Well, let us introduce you to an idea, one we call 'wholeheartedness'. Not 'whole-hearted' as in giving someone whole-hearted support, or committing yourself whole-heartedly to something, because 'wholehearted' is a different thing. Wholehearted describes the state of your heart, it's a condition. To be wholehearted is to be in the position described in today's first paragraph, truly authentic, knowing who we are and who we are meant to be, and responding to life out of that certainty. We'd suggest that wholeheartedness is both a journey and a destination. This last Twenty-Nine days has been the journey. How does one live the destination? We'll unpack that tomorrow, but meanwhile:

Thought Stop and Activation

Can you describe how you're feeling right now? Have you asked your heart how it's feeling recently? As you ask both your head and your heart that question today, see if your heart and heart give the same answer. You may have to ask your heart what lie it's believing

Authenticity is the daily practice of letting go of who you think you're supposed to be and embracing who you actually are; it demands wholehearted living and loving, even when it's hard.

Attributed to Brené Brown

DAY THIRTY

Date

Living the Destination…learning to be authentic

Something we haven't mentioned on any of the last thirty days is love and yet the receiving of love is our most natural desire and need. It's the absence of love that leads to the majority of all the troubles we've been talking about. Immersed in love we'd have been one of those 100 point children; not being loved leads us to think we're unlovable and, ultimately, we can only love others to the degree what we love ourselves. We love ourselves when we reject all the lies we've grown to believe about ourselves as a result of our childhood conditioning and accept ourselves, warts and all, for who and what we are. That's when the authenticity kicks in and we respond to life out of the love we've learned for ourselves.

The idea of being wholehearted includes being authentic, but it means more than just that. Wholeheartedness also includes other behaviours that grow to define us. Empathy is one of these, being able to feel and respond to someone else's pain or distress with no reference to one's own experience, just theirs. Compassion is another, even stronger response, taking empathy and wanting to do something about that pain or distress. There's more though. A balanced approach (homeostasis) based on authenticity and wholeheartedness should seep into and diffuse through to all aspects of our lives, and that includes family, friends, work and play, so we end here with a challenge to you to spend some time thinking about every part of your life and how the new you will cast your vision for it and determine your future…

Thought Stop and Activation*

Here's a list of just some of the areas in life. Take each in turn and apply the questions that follow them:
Your family life
Your marriage / meaningful relationship
Your finances
Your paid work

Your friends
How you look after yourself
Your thought life
How you rest
Your spiritual/prayer life
Your personal growth/skill development

Q1. What obstacles, weaknesses or problems exist in that area?
2. How would you like this area of your life to be?
3. What would be your vision / dream / intention for this area of your life?
4. Can you create a declaration that articulates the outcome of the question above?
5. What is your immediate first step towards achieving vision or dream?
6. What is your ultimate goal?
7. How will you recognise success in achieving that goal?
8. Who will you invite to join you on this new journey?

With many thanks to Paul Manwaring for inspiring this Thought Stop and Activation!

Knowing others is intelligence; knowing yourself is true wisdom.
Lao Tzu

*With many thanks to Paul Manwaring for inspiring this Thought Stop and Activation!

Knowing others is intelligence; knowing yourself is true wisdom.
Lao Tzu

DAY THIRTY-ONE

Date

Finale… "knowing yourself is true wisdom"

Today's title may tell us that it's Day Thirty-One, but it may be week twelve or sixteen in your journey and that's fine! You may have skipped here, to the end, to see if there's a give-away, all Thirty Days explained on half a page, but, sorry, there isn't, it's a journey that has to be lived. On the other hand you may have tracked through day by day, and if you have, we hope that you're happier, wiser and enjoying the freedom that comes with being your true self. It was Lao Tzu who said that "Knowing others is intelligence; knowing yourself is true wisdom", and far be it from us to out-quote Lao Tzu but we'd have to add to this, "and doing something about it", which you, by going through this book, have done. Keep going! Life is a constant process of healing, of identifying those things within us that don't ring true with the 'you' you know you're meant to be and then, by questioning your head and heart, identifying the lie and its origin. Remember too that inner healing is best not done alone. You'll get further quicker with help.

To be the person God intended and made us to be must surely be our ultimate aim and we'd suggest that through inner healing we'll find this in being our truly authentic selves. It was Ralph Waldo Emerson who said that "To be yourself in a world that is constantly trying to make you something else is the greatest accomplishment." And it's mostly true! Again we'd change this slightly to read, "To be yourself in a world that is constantly trying, and has succeeded with most of us, in making us something else, is the greatest accomplishment." Keep chasing authenticity!

We'd love to hear from you! If you have any comments, complaints, thoughts or questions, or if you would like personal help, online or in person, please get in touch! All emails sent to darrell@wonderfullyfree.org will be answered, unless, of course, they're particularly rude, in which case they won't!

Many blessings!
Darrell

Bibliography

The following have contributed to the thinking that produced this book!
'When the Body Says No, the cost of hidden stress' by Gabor Maté
'How to be the Love you Seek' by Dr Nicole LePera
'The Body Keeps the Score' by Bessel van der Kolk
'The Gift of Being Yourself' by David Benner
'Love, Medicine and Miracles' by Bernie Siegel

Also by Darrell Cocup
'Wonderfully Free…no going back'. A 31 day devotional journal for those who have received Sozo inner healing ministry

'Standing Firm…living free'. A 31 day devotional journal for anyone on an inner healing journey

'Wonderfully Free…no going back' is also available in Spanish, German, Dutch and Russian

With Liz Gregg
'The Sozo for Couples Manual'.

'Starting Out…all the questions you should ask before saying , "Yes"'. A marriage preparation manual for couples to work through, with or without a facilitator

'Going Deeper', a 40 day devotional for couples wanting to go deeper with God and each other

All English language titles are available on our website: www.wonderfullyfree.org or from Amazon.

For information or more details contact answers@wonderfullyfree.org

Alpha is a course that explores and explains Christianity, we recommend it highly! Details at www.alpha.org.uk

Printed in Great Britain
by Amazon